First World War
and Army of Occupation
War Diary
France, Belgium and Germany

66 DIVISION
Divisional Troops
Royal Army Medical Corps
1 South African Field Ambulance
1 October 1918 - 31 December 1918

WO95/3132/3

The Naval & Military Press Ltd
www.nmarchive.com
Published in association with The National Archives

Published by

The Naval & Military Press Ltd

Unit 10 Ridgewood Industrial Park,

Uckfield, East Sussex,

TN22 5QE England

Tel: +44 (0) 1825 749494

www.naval-military-press.com

www.nmarchive.com

This diary has been reprinted in facsimile from the original. Any imperfections are inevitably reproduced and the quality may fall short of modern type and cartographic standards.

© **Crown Copyright**
Images reproduced by permission of The National Archives, London, England, 2015.

Contents

Document type	Place/Title	Date From	Date To
Heading	WO95/3132/3		
Heading	B.E.F. 66 Div 1st Sth African Fld Amb 1918 Oct-1919 Feb From 9 Div		
Heading	War Diary of 1st South African Field Ambulance January 1919 Vol 34		
War Diary	Marche Sheet 9 1/100000	01/01/1919	31/01/1919
Heading	War Diary For 1st South African Field Ambulance 66th Division From 1/2/19 To 28/2/19		
War Diary	Marche Sheet 9 Marche 1/100000	01/02/1919	17/02/1919
War Diary	Chateau Tihange Huy	20/02/1919	20/02/1919
War Diary	Sheet 9 (Marche) 1/100,000	24/02/1919	28/02/1919
War Diary	Vauvillers Sheet 17 Amiens	01/10/1918	01/10/1918
War Diary	Montauban	01/10/1918	04/10/1918
War Diary	Combles	04/10/1918	04/10/1918
War Diary	Nurlu	05/10/1918	05/10/1918
War Diary	Ronssoy (Sheet 62.c F.2.ab.6.2)	05/10/1918	07/10/1918
War Diary	Bony (Sheet 62 B) A.15.C.7.8	07/10/1918	10/10/1918
War Diary	Serain	11/10/1918	12/10/1918
War Diary	Maretz (Sheet 57 B)	13/10/1918	18/10/1918
War Diary	Les Folies (Sheet 57 B)	19/10/1918	01/11/1918
War Diary	Maurois Sheet 57 B	02/11/1918	03/11/1918
War Diary	Le Cateau Sheet 57 B	04/11/1918	04/11/1918
War Diary	Pommeruil Sheet 57 B	05/11/1918	05/11/1918
War Diary	Landrecies Sheet 57 B	06/11/1918	06/11/1918
War Diary	Maroilles	07/11/1918	08/11/1918
War Diary	Dompierre	08/11/1918	08/11/1918
War Diary	St Hilaire-Sur-Helpe	09/11/1918	09/11/1918
War Diary	Solre-Le-Chateau (Namur)	10/11/1918	10/11/1918
War Diary	L'Ecrevisse	10/11/1918	10/11/1918
War Diary	Solre-Le-Chateau (Namur Sheet 8)	10/11/1918	17/11/1918
War Diary	Sivry (Namur Sheet 8)	18/11/1918	18/11/1918
War Diary	Senzeille (Namur Sheet 8)	19/11/1918	20/11/1918
War Diary	Philippe Ville (Sheet 8)	23/11/1918	23/11/1918
War Diary	Gochenee (Namur Sheet 8)	24/11/1918	14/12/1918
War Diary	Houyet (Sheet 9 Marche)	14/12/1918	15/12/1918
War Diary	Rochefort (Sheet 9 Marche)	15/12/1918	16/12/1918
War Diary	Marche (Sheet 9)	16/12/1918	31/12/1918

WO 95/3132/3

B. E. F.
66 DIV

1ST STH AFRICAN FLD AMB.
~~1919 JAN & FEB.~~
1918 OCT — 1919 FEB

From 9 DIV

CONFIDENTIAL 96/34

Original
146/5490

WAR DIARY
OF
1ST SOUTH AFRICAN FIELD AMBULANCE
JANUARY 1919.

Jan 1919

COMMITTEE FOR THE
MEDICAL HISTORY OF THE
Date 10 MAR 1919

WAR DIARY
INTELLIGENCE SUMMARY

Army Form C. 2118

Place	Date 1919	Hour	Summary of Events and Information	Remarks and references to Appendices
MARCHE SHEET 9 1/100,000	JAN 1st		Strength of unit 7 Officers 159 Other Ranks.	Authenticated
"	" 15		Capt Oliver S.A.M.C. proceeded for temporary duty with 330 Brigade RFA	
"	" 19		RFA from (tp duty) 9th Gloster Regt. 17 Reinforcements joined unit from S.A. General Hospital ABBEVILLE Ord.	
"	" 25		The unit Horsed Transport & Billets were inspected by Major General H.K. Bethel Cmdg. Div.O. and Lt Col E.G Thackeray Cmdg. R.W. Commanding S.A Brigade Result of Inspection:- 1/1st S.A Field Ambulance headed by 72 place in order of merit out of a total of 81 units in the Division.	
"	" 27		Lieut E.G. Pyott S.A.M.C. reported for duty from South African Military Hospital, Richmond England.	

Army Form C. 2118

WAR DIARY
or
INTELLIGENCE SUMMARY
(Erase heading not required.)

Instructions regarding War Diaries and Intelligence Summaries are contained in F. S. Regs., Part II. and the Staff Manual respectively. Title Pages will be prepared in manuscript.

Place	Date	Hour	Summary of Events and Information	Remarks and references to Appendices
MARCHE Sheet 9 1/100,000	January		Capt E.G. Pyott D.A.M.b proceeded for temporary duty with 100 K.F.A.H. at M.Goofe.	Org
"	" 29th		Owing to Civil regiments the Convent Building which was being used as a Hospital, was evacuated and accommodation for 50 patients was arranged for in the Building located at 7 Rue de la Station Marche	Org
"	" 30th		Col. F.W. Higgo D.O. A.D.M.S. 66 Division inspected the new Hospital.	Org
"	" 31st		Health of unit during month satisfactory. Demobilization progressing slowly. Total number of men demobilized, including attached, during January, NINE. Number of patients in Hospital at 31.1.19. – 118. Strength of unit 7 Officers & 217 Other Ranks.	Org

O.J. Myfle
Lt. Col.
C.O. 1st SOUTH AFRICAN FIELD AMBULANCE

MEDICAL

WO 35

Confidential.

WAR DIARY.

— FOR —

1st South African Field Ambulance.

66th Division.

From 1/2/19.

To 28/2/19.

WAR DIARY
or
INTELLIGENCE SUMMARY

Army Form C. 2118

Place	Date	Hour	Summary of Events and Information	Remarks and references to Appendices
MARCHE SHEET 9 MARCHE 1/100,000	FEB 1st		Strength of unit 7 Officers & 219 Other Ranks.	enough Heavy
"	2nd		4 Other Ranks represented the S.A.Field Amb. in Civilian celebrations to returned Belgian Soldiers	AJ
"	7th		5 Other Ranks escorts returned to England for demobilization	AJ
"	8th		Capt. A.J. Wallis D.M.O. joined unit from N.O. Gen. Hospital	AJ
"	10th		Capt. G.B. Lennessy proceeded for temp duty to 330 Brigade R.F.A.	
"			Capt. S.B. Clewer returned from temp duty at 330 Brigade R.F.A.	
"			2/Capt F.M. Pringle N.D.M.O. & Capt. S.B. Clewer proceeded to form with South African Rugby Touring team.	
"			Major M.I. Power A.D. took over duties of O.C unit during Lt Col Hughes absence	
"	13th		General De St. Fou Luis Botha inspected the S.A. Brigade & after addressed the men. Text of remarks attached.	AJ

Army Form C. 2118

WAR DIARY
or
INTELLIGENCE SUMMARY
(Erase heading not required.)

Instructions regarding War Diaries and Intelligence Summaries are contained in F.S. Regs., Part II. and the Staff Manual respectively. Title Pages will be prepared in manuscript.

Place	Date	Hour	Summary of Events and Information	Remarks and references to Appendices
MARCHE SPEC. Q (MARCHE) 1/100,000	16TH		Major Davis S.O. Acting O.O. proceeded to England for demobilization. Capt. B.G. Cyatt 2nd M.O. returned from 14 days duty at 100 Batt M.G. Corps. In accordance with instructions received from A.N. 20 Brigade + ADMS obtaining the transport of the unit proceeded to a new M.T. Lng area. Owing to slippery condition of roads it moved light.	App
"	17TH		2/oc A.M. Bungle + Capt. B.G. Clover rejoined unit from Paris in accordance with instructions received from ADMS 20th div. the unit moved, under orders of 20 Brigade, by Motor Lories to the CHATEAU TIHANGE NEAR HUY. Map Ref. MARCHE SHEET No 9. 1/100,000. and opened a Brigade HospL at the Chateau. Capt A.J. Rollo 3rd M.O. invalided sick to C.C.S.	App
CHATEAU TIHANGE N.N.	20TH			
SHEET 9 (MARCHE) 1/100,000	24TH		Col Biggs + DMS + both Sir visited the unit + inspected the Hospital	App
"	28TH		The first weekly quota of 10 O/Ranks proceeded to England for demobilization. Strength B/Unit 5 Officers (S.A.M.C.) and 143 O/Ranks (included Heart Station Ambulance + dental + Laboratory. Thinks O/patients in hospital at date. — 144 O/Ranks.	App

ORTrimple
LT. COL.,
C.B. 1ST SOUTH AFRICAN FIELD AMBULANCE

WAR DIARY

INTELLIGENCE SUMMARY
(Erase heading not required.)

Place	Date 1916	Hour	Summary of Events and Information	Remarks and references to Appendices
VAUVILLERS (nr AMIENS)	Oct 1	08.15	Strength of Medical Personnel 9 Officers 167 O'Ranks. Orders for the Unit to move from VAUVILLERS were received at 02.45. The unit to be on the road at 08.15. The packing of wagons was immediately proceeded with, as most of that had been unpacked for the purpose of establishing a Rest Station. Notwithstanding the order the Ambulance was on the road at 08.15 and proceeded to MONTAUBAN via short route.	Dr Trungh
MONTAUBAN	" 1	15.30	MONTAUBAN by march route completing the move at 15.30. Immediately upon arrival the establishing of a Field Hospital, for the reception of the sick of the Brigade was proceeded with, same being in the sunken road running between MONTAUBAN and MARICOURT. Captain A.G. FORBES M.C. S.A.M.C. evacuated to C.C.S. suffering from an Accidental injury (HAND & SICK). Captain J.M. N. RICHARDSON returned from leave to the U.K.	O.T. A.T.
"	" 4		The Ambulance moved off from MONTAUBAN by march route at 10.00 and proceeded to COMBLES arriving at 12.30 and at 19.30 moved off	A.T.
COMBLES	" 4	12.30	proceeded to NURLU where it arrived at 01.30. At 10.00 the	
NURLU	" 5	01.30	again proceeding to FONSSOY (sheet 62c	
FONSSOY Sheet 62c F20 F5.2	" 5	14.00	F.20.F.5.d) at 14.00. Captain E.H. OLIVER S.A.M.C. applied for duty from South African Military Hospital RICHMOND.	A.T.
"	" 7		The Division moved up to-day and in accordance with 66th Div. Medical Arrangements to this Fd Ambulance I was placed in charge of the evacuation of the wounded from the forward Area, having at my disposal 2 Officers & Pers. Ligeries, four large Motor Ambulances and one Ford 1 Mte 2/2 E. Lance Field Ambulance and 1 Officer Bearer Division, one Cafe Car and one Ford of the 2/3 East Lancs Field Ambulance in attached to my own. Personnel in accordance with Arrangement	A.T.

WAR DIARY
INTELLIGENCE SUMMARY
(Erase heading not required.)

Instructions regarding War Diaries and Intelligence Summaries are contained in F.S. Regs., Part II. and the Staff Manual respectively. Title pages will be prepared in manuscript.

Army Form C.2118.

Place	Date 1918	Hour	Summary of Events and Information	Remarks and references to Appendices
BONY March 21 A.15 C.7.8	Oct 8		There was also a short-wheel FORD Car for forward work at those on my return at the Collecting Point BELLEVIEW, in command of Cars was held up. Account of heavy shellfire. Army units by M.A.D.M.S. who made two attempts. No.10 M.A.C. Cars at Cars were sparsely unused.	O/S
"	9		On the ground the Surgeons with Dressing Parties Dressers at BONY. A front- line Station with one Officer worked the Posts. This should be noticed, the M.O. reported to me for duty. All day did not come. Sufficient numbers to allow Surgeons at any time. Evacuation of Cases to C.C.S. was carried out by the No. 10 M.A.C. and the number of Ambulances was sufficient to ope with the requirements. No strategic effort was found necessary to establish M.D.S.	O/S
"	10	10.00	Forward Post was cleared at BONY at Noon. 10 instant Everything at U.14.F.6.6. (East of SERAIN) at the same Hour by 90 2/2 East Anglian Ambulance. At Estrées Les Crecy & Sub. Tapestries Hankils and Shoten also carrying a Medical Comforts Van at BONY on the evening of to the O/C 2/2 E.A. Field Amb. As from Noon 10 instant supervision of work in the Area in front of the M.D.S came under the orbit of the No 2/2 Eastern Field Ambulance who also sent the Surgeons Cars from under any Charge, M.A.C. Cars and Lorries. So soon as	O/S
"	10	12.00	At BONY was cleared (about 12.00) my N.Co and Principal, with no Tent out Equipment moved to SERAIN to await further orders.	O/S
SERAIN	11		Captain J. DEV MEIRING injured army leave for U.K. from C.C.5	O/S
"	12		Captain A.G FORBES Mc proceeded to U.K. for duty with the South African Hospital RICHMOND.	O/S

A.3534 Wt. W.4973 M687 730,000 8/16 D.D. & L.Ltd. Forms/C.2118/13.-

WAR DIARY or INTELLIGENCE SUMMARY

Place: MARETZ (Sheet 57B)
Date: Oct 13 1918

MAJOR POWER'S REPORT (CONT'D)

"November with the assistance of 21st M.A.C. and a place of my disposal by the
"D.D.M.S. XIII Corps. The difficulty was ammunition and the transport situation. The
"Undertaking of the A.D.M.S. 66 Div. MONT ST MARTIN was impossible. Ultimately
"the Q.A. and a temporary A.D.S. was opened at SERAIN, cases being collected
"at a Car Post established at AVELUCOURT owing to this being the
"advance and a temporary M.O. French was placed with the T.M.O.S. (?) of the
"Lancers who reports the evacuation. I was not unmindful of unsuccessful
"but a considerable number of cases were collected and evacuated. During the
"day. Eventually the casualties were few. Early the morning of
"10th. Much was the continuation with all R.M.O's by Capt JARVIS and Capt
"the holding of a position along the MAURAIS a casualty post was established
"at the many crossings first met by the village. A little later an excellent
"site was found in the village A.D. (Sunday) which was in a [illegible]
"hospital by the Germans and the Q.M.S. was satisfactory [illegible] as a
"became established for the time, no difficulty was experienced with collection
"evacuation of cases, and all casualty clearances were handled
"well and smoothly. As at ST MARTIN all twelve Motor Ambulances were
"accommodated at the A.D.S. more numerous Ambulances accommodation were
"On Aug 13th thanks to the A.D.S. & T.M. Corps B.Nos 2/3 & [illegible] Field Amb.
"and rejoined my Unit at MARITZ.

REPORT OF WORK OF STRETCHER BEARERS OF 6th DIVISION By Capt. H.R. LAURENCE

"On the 7th instant I was put in charge of the Stretcher Bearers of the three
"Field Ambulances and I made a reconnaissance of the whole
"Divisional Area from when we were taking over until I got the personnel

WAR DIARY / INTELLIGENCE SUMMARY

Place	Date	Hour	Summary of Events and Information	Remarks and references to Appendices
MAREITZ (Sheet 57 B)	Oct 13 1918		Capt Lawrence's report continued:—	

"R.A.Ps and Bearer Posts & arranged additional relay Posts. The attempt to get in touch with T.M.Bs before they moved to forward area to support the infantry attack had not time to do this for more than two of them.
"On the final casualties were evacuated through the Bearer Posts arranged by the Bearer posts & later by the day BELLEVUE FARM whereas the Car evacuating Post & by the Surgeon from which all casualties were evacuated to A.D.S. MONT ST MARTIN by car.
"The casualties by R.M.O. going forward to the T.A.Ps & later attacks. were also reaching the T.A.Ps without letting us know their wants Posts.
"On the Rt. Brigade advanced so quickly that it was imperative at first to keep in touch with the Regiments. No one came to the R.M.O. has under the circumstances of the fighting no post R.A.P.
"At the start the Advance on this day to Car Collecting post was at the PLAT FOLIE & FARM, and later at AVELY and the A.D.S situated "at SERAIN in default of a better position further forward.
"Collected by accruing thousands behind. Casualties were Major Motor Ambulances. All casualties were got to A.D.S remarkably "On the 10th. a Car Collecting post was made at the "next morning.
"N.A.D.S. was established behind MAUROIS temporarily soon afterwards "up the MAUROIS – LE CATEAU Road at MAUROIS & Relay Bearer posts were placed "Cross Roads along the track into the Valley bearing to the right & more "directly towards LE CATEAU. All casualties were mainly first morning.
"On 14.Oct all T.A.Ps were moved locations by Map References further relay Post was placed at the main Cross Roads West of LE CATEAU. From this day

WAR DIARY
INTELLIGENCE SUMMARY

Place	Date	Hour	Summary of Events and Information	Remarks and references to Appendices
MARETZ (Sheet 57B)	Oct 13 /1918		May 14 Gen, one tent sub section, and transport moved from SERAIN by March Route at 11:00 to MARETZ, to await further orders.	
			REPORT BY MAJOR M.S. POWER, D.S.O. S.A.M.C. on WORK AT A.D.S. 7th/15th inclusive.	
			"On the morning of the 7th instant, I proceeded under orders to MONT-ST-MARTIN with my sub section and established an A.D.S. at the CHATEAU making arrangements for the accommodation of all ranks, and recce the forward area. Captain LEVISEUR went forward to recommend the 182 Cy RE's Headquarters, whilst Captain RIOTT remained with me. On 8th Cpty of the 182 Cy RE's headquarters accompanied in cleaning out and doing further repair of the building, and by 18:00 we were ready for the reception of cases. Arrangements were made for trusting between the stay tents and the ADS. He main car Pat was situated at BONY, when also was the walking wounded collection Pat. Out M.O. for R.W.W. Posts were also available. Lt Col PRINGLE visited the ADS later, that same nine were available. The first cases arrived about 23:00 on the 7th and from that time... by arrival in a steady stream during the night. Horse ambulances were brought from the ADS to and behind BEAU RENOIR. Attack began to arrive about an hour after the 8:30 (bombardment) and the other immediately on ____ day and up to about 01:00 on the morning of 9th. Immediate the last case.— wounded German prisoners — arrive at 02:30 on the 9th. "All cases have been evacuated and the ___ resumed ___ Evacuation was carried on mostly until the afternoon owing to a block in the traffic at the cross roads near Mont St Martin, and then ___ of the 8th was impossible, the cases away and there — an accumulation of the sick. Passage at the A.D.S.	Oct 13

WAR DIARY
INTELLIGENCE SUMMARY
(Erase heading not required.)

Place	Date 1918	Hour	Summary of Events and Information	Remarks and references to Appendices
MARETZ Sheet 57B	Oct 1 18		Capt Lawrence's Report continued. "Day until the 16th instant all RAPs were visited & located daily, all casualties were evacuated without delay. When necessary Ford Cars were used for collecting pnt. On the 16th Oct was relieved by Major FERGUSON 2/3 East Lancs Field Ambulance, after being shown round all the RAPs by the same Division in area.	
	16	06.00	On 16th instant 9/C 2/3 East Lancs Field Ambulance assumed responsibility for the evacuation of the forward area. One car stationed at Cabaret MEUNIER Lorien Advanced car Horse Ambulance and bearers being detailed H. FORD returned from Corps & Mt Ambulance ran to Field Ambulance on 9/7 tick. Capt Mc JOHNS same being M.O. for N. South African Company Heg as M.O.	
	18		One other car took tech deputy up to limited the 90 to build ambulance at 07.30 am as the following day in accordance with instructions received from 4/63 MT MACETZ to see Forces and found G. to 15.90 hours. The C. in C. was relieved of all cases Mt points.	
LES FOLIES Sheet 57B	19			
	20	06.00		
	21		Casualty had ambulance at ..... being carried at all rail head ... evacuation of wounded for evacuation to points ...	

WAR DIARY
INTELLIGENCE SUMMARY
(Erase heading not required.)

Place	Date	Hour	Summary of Events and Information	Remarks and references to Appendices
Lesfosses Oct B	Oct 31 1918		Captain E.G. Bott S.A.M.C. proceeded to Rio Louis Base for temporary duty as R.M.O. in relief of Captain E.U. Lewis-Enright who proceeded on leave to the U.K. for 14 days from 2/11/18. Strength: Medical bearers & Unit Officers 162 N.C.Os.	

A. Smyth Lt Col
S.A.M.C.
O/c. 1st SOUTH AFRICAN FIELD AMBULANCE

WAR DIARY
INTELLIGENCE SUMMARY

(Erase heading not required.)

Army Form C. 2118

Place	Date 1918	Hour	Summary of Events and Information	Remarks and references to Appendices
LES FOLIES SHEET 57 B	Nov 1		Strength of Unit. 9 Officers. 163 Other Ranks.	
"	2	10.00	In conjunction with the advancing troops, the Division moved forward to the 25th Division, the ambulance in turn to Maurois by march route and complete there at 12.30.	
MAUROIS SHEET 57 B	2	13.30	Moving to MAUROIS by march route and complete there new Mounds & LE	
"	3		On the following day the unit moved to	
LE CATEAU SHEET 57 B	4		CATEAU. Strength at 16.00 a.m. on 4th	
"			Major R.S. POWER DSO in charge A.D.S.	
"			POMMEREUIL established an A.D.S.	
"			Evacuation of wounded carried on from	
"	5		(illegible)	
POMMEREUIL SHEET 57 B		At 10.30 a.m. 13.30 a.m.		
"	6	6.00		
LANDRECIES Sheet 57 B				
"				
MARQILLES	7	10.00		
"	7	10.00		

WAR DIARY
INTELLIGENCE SUMMARY
(Erase heading not required.)

Army Form C. 2118

Place	Date	Hour	Summary of Events and Information	Remarks and references to Appendices
ST HILAIRE SUR-HELPE	Nov 9		At 17.15 hours information was received that the enemy column was retiring to the North and that the 15 Lancers were rushing to intercept them. A mobile column was organised under the command of Brig-Gen TANNER consisting of forces such as he can get two Infantry Coys, 1 Bde RFA and 1 sect 4.5" Hy 1430 H Coy B Div Coy, 1 Coy Motor M.G. Bn., 1 Sqn 12th Lancers, New Zed Ambulance, Mobile Vety & more lorried journeys. He moves forward orders to mop up resistance & reinforce units for army - the Bdes who left to take up position 2/3rd Cdn Field Ambulance joined forces with my Ambulance at 18.00 hours, accompanied by my lorries transport. Two motor barcoms, [?] cars. The two field ambulances were to two [a?] atab ford cars. The Hy [?] accompany us on account of the bad state of the roads. He being unable to negotiate in the dark. He to be left in charge of Capt SAMPSON MO S.M.O. was also joined at dawn next morning. In accordance with my orders from the Gen TANNER I proceeded to SOLRE-LE-CHATEAU where I arrived after 12 hours on the road. The [?] were on repair work, bridges, obstacles etc, having been up by the retiring enemy detains across country at this place.	

Army Form C. 2118

WAR DIARY
or
~~INTELLIGENCE SUMMARY~~

(Erase heading not required.)

Instructions regarding War Diaries and Intelligence Summaries are contained in F. S. Regs., Part II. and the Staff Manual respectively. Title Pages will be prepared in manuscript.

Place	Date	Hour	Summary of Events and Information	Remarks and references to Appendices
SOLRE-LE-CHATEAU (NAMUR SHEET 8)	1918 Nov 10		to wounded, evacuating cases to the [illegible] where [illegible] evacuated them to the [illegible] D.S. [illegible] motor ambulance car. [illegible] post all clear of cases, [illegible] evacuated to the M.D. Station.	[illegible]
"	" 11		At 10.30 the following [illegible] was received:- "Hostilities will cease at 11.00 hours today [illegible] "[illegible] line reached at that hour [illegible] "to Advanced Army H.Q. [illegible] "There will be no intercourse with the enemy [illegible] "Instructions from Army H.Qrs. [illegible]" These tidings were immediately communicated to [illegible] being received quietly and without [illegible]. [illegible] carried out as usual, discipline being relaxed [illegible] reason of the cessation of hostilities.	[illegible]
"	" 12		Capt. A H GIFFORD S.A.M.C. relieved of his duties [illegible] in charge of the XIII Corps Reception Camp [illegible] No 1 South African General Hospital for duty.	[illegible]
"	" 15		66th Division transferred to IX Corps from 12 noon [illegible]	[illegible]
"	" 17		Captain E H CLUVER S.A.M.C. returned from [illegible] duty with 331 Brigade R.F.A. In accordance with the terms of the Armistice, occupied portions of FRANCE BELGIUM and LUXEMBURG are to be evacuated by the 26th Nov. 18.	

1875 Wt. W593/826 1,000,000 4/15 J.B.C. & A. A.D.S.S./Forms/C. 2118.

WAR DIARY
INTELLIGENCE SUMMARY
(Erase heading not required.)

Army Form C. 2118

Place	Date	Hour	Summary of Events and Information	Remarks and references to Appendices
SOLRE-LE-CHATEAU	Nov 17		The advance of the Allied Forces commenced on the 17th inst. beginning with the advance on NAMUR. The Xth Corps was preceded by the 2nd Cav. Division on the march to the line NAMUR-DINANT. The ambulance moved from SOLRE-LE-CHATEAU at 12:30 hours, arriving at SIVRY at 15:30	
NANUL SHEET 6	18	15:30	en route to SIVRY. No new cases. The ambulance procuring billets in the village.	
SIVRY NAMUR Nov 5	18		Lt. Hal. Molden procuring cases for ambulance arrival at SIVRY. Moderate reception to the sick. M.H. He Caro attached for the journey. Nos. Capt. W. M. H. Clifton N.L., C.C.S. Bohan, W. M. H. Le Caro came on the march.	
SENZEILLE NAMUR SHEET Y	19	10:00	Everything being continued to SENZEILLE. At 10:00 hours the march was continued to SENZEILLE. The filled ambulance arrived at 15:30 hours. Whilst the village, the inhabitants. Billets in the village the inhabitants were very enthusiastic and all they could do for the men, succeeding their houses being at their disposal. Many of the men slept in beds for the first time since leaving their homes as the last billets. It was continued here as three days here.	
	20		Capt. E H LENISEUR S.A.M.C. returned from leave to the U.K.	
PHILIPPEVILLE NAMUR SHEET 5	23 09:00		The furniture moved from SENZEILLE to PHILIPPEVILLE starting at 09:00 hrs and completing the day's march at 11:30, and arriving at 10 o'clock. At PHILIPPEVILLE Dinner in again for the night.	
COCHENEE NAMUR SHEET 8	24 10:00		COCHENEE at 14:30. Here again the unit was the first billeted unit to be billeted in the village, a great enthusiasm reception by the inhabitants.	

Army Form C. 2118

INTELLIGENCE SUMMARY
(Erase heading not required.)

Instructions regarding War Diaries and Intelligence Summaries are contained in F.S. Regs., Part II and the Staff Manual respectively. Title Pages will be prepared in manuscript.

Place	Date 1915	Hour	Summary of Events and Information	Remarks and references to Appendices
GOCHENE & NAMUR) Mar 8	Mar 27		Capt. B. Sampson. M.C. S.A.M.C. proceeded to X Coys Reception Camp for temporary duty, a notification having received to the effect that in consequence of practically all men of 5 Mountain Battery Division went practically to camp, that welfare of officers were taken to camp much impaired. Major M.S. Power. D.S.O. 2 Lieut. Colonel Officer, with the Service Army School Basic will. French Matthews. English Dutch Pharkness and Banking the following...	
"	28		...	
"	30		Capt. E.G. Roth reported for... Lieut. F.J. van den Bergh...	

[Signature] Lt. Col.
O.C. 1st SOUTH AFRICAN FIELD AMBULANCE

WAR DIARY
INTELLIGENCE SUMMARY
(Erase heading not required.)

Army Form C. 2118

Place	Date	Hour	Summary of Events and Information	Remarks and references to Appendices
MARCHE (See 9)	Mar 24		A Hospital was opened in the morning for the reception of sick from the South African Brigade. These were mostly convalescents from the influenza epidemic, but included a few cases of influenza and some of pneumonia. The Hospital was conducted as a Rest Station for Class II from which patients were evacuated to Base as occasion arose. Officers & men of the Brigade also reported sick as required and were dealt with & evacuated through the usual channels.	
	25		The morning was spent in the search for a suitable site for the new Hospital. Buildings were examined at Hun, Lt Col R N Pringle (Pl 90) returned to duty. Lt Col Clover DSO M.O. i/c M.S. POWER RAMC went to Hun. Bathing parades were attended & fatigue parties employed in the usual way in preparation for the removal of the Hospital.	
	26		Capt. D. SIMPSON M.C. proceeded on leave to the U.K. from the 9/2/17 to 10/11/1/F.	a.J
	27		H.R.H. the PRINCE OF WALES inspected the South African Field Ambulance being en route to part of the Brigade.	a.J
	28		Capt E.H. CLOVER proceeded to the J. Glascock Red Lamsbury Bd. Lt Col R N PRINGLE DSO M.O. returned from duty as RAMC. in Command of the Ambulance.	
	31		Strength: 9 Officers. 159 Other ranks.	

A. Pringle LT. COL.,
I.C. 1st SOUTH AFRICAN FIELD AMBULANCE